IMAGES
of America

MEDINA LAKE

Straddling the county line between Medina County and Bandera County, Medina Lake has hosted sailing regattas, speedboat races, and fishing tournaments as well as swimming, scuba diving, and snorkeling. While its heyday was after World War II when this map was published, its white limestone bottom and pure waters continue to entice locals and tourists to enjoy the deep, cool waters and fresh gulf breezes. (Courtesy of the Frontier Times Museum.)

ON THE COVER: Amidst a jumble of canoes in 1915, swimmers survey the aqua, crystal clear waters soon after they rose to fill Medina Lake. While bathing costumes have changed with time, the lake's appeal has remained unchanged. Whether it's a hot summer day or a warm winter afternoon, there is natural beauty and peace of mind at Medina Lake all year long. (Courtesy of the Seekatz family.)

IMAGES
of America

MEDINA LAKE

Rebecca Huffstutler Norton and
Karen Downing Ripley

ARCADIA
PUBLISHING

Published by Arcadia Publishing
Charleston, South Carolina

Library of Congress Control Number: 2011940632

For all general information, please contact Arcadia Publishing:
Telephone 843-853-2070
Fax 843-853-0044
E-mail sales@arcadiapublishing.com
For customer service and orders:
Toll-Free 1-888-313-2665

Visit us on the Internet at www.arcadiapublishing.com

CONTENTS

ACKNOWLEDGMENTS

A Medina Lake waterfront resident and business owner for over 30 years, Karen Ripley is currently serving a second term as vice president of the Bandera County River Authority and Groundwater District. Rebecca Huffstutler Norton serves as the executive director of the Frontier Times Museum in Bandera, Texas. The authors have many to thank whose dedication, expertise, and assistance have made this book possible. They are incredibly grateful to Janie Bourquin, who shared the Seekatz family photographs that trace the lake's history from her grandmother's stroll on the newly built Medina Dam to her family's lakeside businesses; to Tom and Kristina Fett, who shared the legacy of Kris's grandmother, Panchita Thomson, whose drive and enthusiasm helped build Lakehills; to Dan and Loy Ed Johnson Alanis, Ronnie and Bobbie Jo Basinger, and Bobby and Patty Harris, who worked hard to build a community that serves the lake's residents. All three gentlemen have served as county commissioners. Thanks go to Merry Langlinais and County Commissioner Doug King for their efforts to preserve the story of the construction of Medina Dam.

Marlene Leibold Grotheus opened her family album and brought the rough-and-tumble early days to life for us. Thank you, to Burgin and Valli Johnson, whose stories and love of the lake has made it a special place for the Norton family. The family of Joe Granieri—Chris and Debbie Heyen and Cappy Phillips—lent their photographs of places that brought so much joy to so many lake-goers. A visit to Bradford Boehme on a rainy afternoon after a summertime of devastating drought seemed appropriate as he told the story of his family—the Habys, Seekatzes, and Boehmes, whose lives intertwine through the lake's history.

Thank-yous go to the Bandera County River Authority and Groundwater District for its continued vigilance to protect the waters of Bandera County; to Bob Caswell and Barbara Engel of the Lakehills Betterment Association; and to Robert and Barbara Brischetto and Don and Sharon Sloan of LAMCOS and the Medina River Protection Fund and Clean-Up project. Thank-yous also go to Amy Fulkerson and Shellie Eagan of the Witte Museum, Tom Shelton at UTSA's Institute of Texan Cultures, Heather Ferguson of the Marion Koogler McNay Art Museum, and Burt Spoerl for assisting with our research.

A special thank-you goes to Ann and John Dale, Ralph Dresser, and Jane Alberthal for sharing their vast knowledge of the history of the lake. Special gratitude goes to Rev. Cyril Matthew Kuehne, SM; Dorothy Alatorre; and Marilyn J. Schiltz whose books served as our guide. The authors would like to thank the Medina Lake Preservation Society and the board of trustees and staff of the Frontier Times Museum for their encouragement and support. And finally, a thank-you to Mayor Ruby Vera of Natalia, Texas; Gary Cox; Leonard Moore; Alex Watson's daughter Mary Helen Tassos; and the many families, organizations, and businesses who took the time to share their photographs and memories. It was a pleasure and an honor to be a part of your history.

Unless otherwise noted, all photographs in chapters two and three are courtesy of Ed Burger and the Bexar, Medina, Atascosa Water Improvement District No. 1.

INTRODUCTION

Medina Lake is a very special place that was born of a fantastic dream—a dream as big as Texas that ultimately took the tenacity, skill, and imagination of a cast of thousands. And, like many ambitious dreams, the cost of bringing it into reality ran high. The crystal clear waters of Medina Lake belie the controversy that has plagued the body of water since its inception and creation when a group of developers saw the potential to build a dam, creating a lake that could be used to irrigate farmlands to the south. The waters of Medina Lake flow from the Medina River, which has a long history of providing sustenance to those who have lived and traveled along its banks. Before the Europeans landed on the shores of the New World, early Native Americans hunted along the riverbanks and used the caves high in the limestone bluffs above the river as shelter. Later, the Lipan Apaches set up their camps to take advantage of the vast resources of fish, pecans, and wildlife. In 1854, the river would be the site of an early settlement of Mormons who settled at the base of a bluff that came to be known as Mormon's Bluff. After the Civil War, herds of cattle from South Texas followed the Medina River on their way to the Western Trail that brought cattle north to the markets in the Midwest.

Families came and settled along the river to farm its fertile riverbanks, graze cattle, and raise goats and sheep along the rocky limestone outcroppings. But farmers and ranchers in Texas have always been at the mercy of harsh droughts and devastating floods. The need for irrigation was an early concern. In the 1840s, before the arrival of the Mormons, Henri Castro, French impresario and founder of Castroville, explored this area and saw that the Medina River could be used for irrigation for his colony's farms if there were a way to contain the periodic floods that rushed through the canyons the river flowed through.

It was not until 1894 that this observation would be acted upon by a young man from San Antonio named Alex Walton. While on a hunting expedition in Box Canyon, Walton saw the potential of capturing the Medina's floodwaters in the canyon. His belief in a future dam was so strong and the magnitude of the scheme so bewildering that he committed himself to the study of engineering. It took 17 years before he could begin to bring his idea into fruition. Walton and fellow engineers Terrell Bartlett and Willis Ranney sought funding to make their dream a reality, and in 1910 they met Dr. Frederick Pearson, an American engineer involved in dam projects in North and South America, who had the ability to find the needed investors. Pearson successfully raised $6 million through British investors to finance the construction of the Medina Dam and irrigation project. The Medina Irrigation Company was formed and filed for the appropriation of the Medina River waters to be used for irrigation from the watersheds of Bandera and Medina Counties. Construction of the dam began in November 1911 and was completed only a year later in November 1912. At the time, the concrete dam was the largest dam in Texas and the fourth-largest in the United States. Dunlay, Rio Medina, and Castroville joined the newly formed towns of Mico, named for the Medina Irrigation Company (MICO), and Natalia, named for Dr. Pearson's daughter, which arose to provide services for the laborers and a headquarters for the farms to come.

The lake came at a price for many ranchers and farmers who had established their homesteads and ranches on land that was destined to be flooded by the lake. The lake was completed before condemnation proceedings were concluded, as many ranchers not only protested the price offered for their valuable bottom lands along the river but also the entire prospect of losing their way of life for the benefit of others far to the south below the dam. Dr. Pearson ordered that no lands be sold below the dam before the water was available to irrigate the crops that would come. This delay was costly because upon the lake's completion, the Medina Irrigation Company had to wait a year and a half before 125 feet of water was behind the dam and the irrigation system was ready to carry water to the farms. With the advent of World War I and the loss of Dr. Pearson aboard the *Lusitania*, prospects for the successful development of the farms below the dam were dramatically diminished. However, fortunes above the dam improved as travelers flocked to the blue-green waters to swim, boat, fish, and escape the heat of cities and towns. The former farmers and ranchers who retained the land above the lake's shoreline adapted by catering to their needs.

Access to the lake was limited to a few poor roads. Local businessmen such as Joe Granieri and Frank Seekatz built their own roads, cleverly directing traffic to their camps, lodges, and marinas. The Angler's Club and a variety of San Antonio civic organizations successfully launched a mass appeal for construction of a state highway to Medina Lake from San Antonio via an existing toll road. Avalon Ranch developer Lester Whipple donated land to the state for a park in order to justify the Angler's Club's push for a state highway. With the construction of these new roads, people who had come only for the weekends now were able to make the trip to and from San Antonio in a single day. This was the heyday of the lake, when legendary places such as Camp Medina, Joe's Place, Fred's Dam Place, Whitley's, Leibold Fishing Camp, and Goathill Camp were established to cater to sportsmen, the wealthy, families, and even soldiers from nearby San Antonio. Water lovers began looking to build their homes in paradise, and neighborhoods like Pebble Beach, Lake Medina Highlands, and the majestic-sounding Avalon (named for the lake's dragon shape) were developed. Splendid homes built high on the limestone bluffs above the lake brought both the famous and the infamous, and the lake became home to many legendary characters.

As other lakes were built throughout Texas and as extended droughts became more a way of life, Medina Lake saw a decline in its water levels and the number of tourists who came to enjoy its pristine waters. Water resources continue to be threatened, and the residents of the lake often find themselves at odds with the agencies controlling the flow of water from the lake to the farmlands south of the dam as well as to the sprawling city of San Antonio. To address these concerns, groups such as the Medina Lake Betterment Association, Lake Medina Conservation Society (LAMCOS), the Medina River Protection Fund, and the Medina Lake Preservation Society continue working together passionately to preserve this gem of the Texas Hill Country. Through all of this, the communities of Lakehills and Mico have become well-established and continue to develop and grow with a diverse mix of residents, ranging from weekenders and snowbirds to commuters and retirees, all escaping the city for the peaceful beauty and tranquility of Medina Lake and small-town life.

One

LIFE BEFORE THE DAM

Before there was a lake, the Medina River flowed through a valley rich in pecan and cypress trees and encompassed by hills and limestone bluffs. The river played a pivotal role in the settlement of Texas. The cypress trees gave rise to the industries of shingle making and charcoal burning, while the abundant resources of the river provided sustenance to those who settled and traveled the area. (Courtesy of Rebecca Norton.)

The caves around Medina River were once used by prehistoric inhabitants who were seasonal hunter-gatherers. The caves provided shelter and protection, while the abundance of wildlife fed and clothed them. In historic times, a variety of Indian tribes occupied the area, including the Lipan Apaches, who camped on the riverbanks to gather pecans and wild plums and take advantage of the plentiful fish and game. (Courtesy of the Seekatz family.)

French-born Henri Castro negotiated with Republic of Texas president Sam Houston to bring 600 families to settle in the Republic of Texas. The families were recruited from the French region of Alsace and were of German descent. Beginning in 1843, colonies were established near or along the river. Each family was promised an allotment of land when a home was built and at least 15 acres were under cultivation. (Courtesy of the Castroville Chamber of Commerce.)

In 1854, Elder Lyman Wight and his colony of about 250 Mormons arrived in Bandera on the Medina River. After migrating from Illinois to Texas to escape persecution, they soon moved 12 miles downstream. Settling along the river, they named their settlement Mountain Valley. The colonists were skilled farmers and furniture makers, selling their wares in Castroville and San Antonio. Today, the site is known as Mormon's Bluff. (Courtesy of Karen Downing Ripley.)

While the area offered freshwater and game, the colony did not last long. Under constant attack by Indians, Elder Wight (seen here with his wife) wrote to the authorities in Austin, pleading for protection: "This is their former hunting ground where they found all kinds of game in abundance . . . and in as much as the government sells this land to immigrants they ought to protect them." After Wight's sudden death in 1858, the colony disbanded. (Courtesy of the Frontier Times Museum.)

After the Civil War, cattle from South Texas were driven across the Medina River through Bandera County on their way to the Western Trail, the principal thoroughfare to drive cattle to markets in the Midwest. These two cowboys are pictured taking a break in the area of Medina River that would later be the site of the Medina Lake. (Courtesy of Kristina and Tom Fett.)

A successful cattle operation was carried on at Ten-Mile Crossing on the Medina River by Louis Schorp and his brothers-in-law John and Joseph Spettel. By 1881, John and his wife, Theresa Leibold, were living in this home south of Mitchell's Crossing on the Medina River. Upon completion of the Medina Dam, the house was moved to its present location at Thousand Trails Resort before the lake waters rose. (Courtesy of Medina Lake Thousand Trails.)

Between 1860 and 1870, Alsatian, Polish, and German settlers from nearby towns began to move into the fertile river valley to farm and raise cattle. The Boehme family retained their farm in Rio Medina, but in 1876 Armin Boehme acquired additional land on the river for raising cattle. Here, Armin poses with his family. Adolf and Henry, pictured to Armin's right, tended to the cattle when they were older. (Courtesy of Bradford Boehme.)

Adolph Boehme raised cattle at the family ranch with his brother Henry and cousin Charles. Henry and Charles did what they called their "batching" at the river. As bachelors, they lived in the rock shelters in the bluffs and used the walls of the canyon as their cattle pens. Since one was left-handed and one was right-handed, they could round the cattle up and rope from either side. (Courtesy of Bradford Boehme.)

Among the original Alsatian colonists were John Leibold I and his wife, Theresa. They settled first in the Haby Settlement near Castroville where their son John Jr. was born. In 1882, John Jr. and his brother-in-law Anton Baetz established the Leibold Ranch near the Medina River. It was a wild and remote area where Indians often raided the ranch to steal horses. (Courtesy of Marlene Leibold Grothues.)

Anton Leibold, eldest son of John Leibold Jr., built a home for his bride, Annie Zinsmeister, in a pecan bottom halfway between a spring and the Medina River. Anton raised horses to sell to the government, and for extra money the family picked pecans from the trees along the river until they filled a big wagon. They would drive for two days to reach San Antonio to sell the pecans. (Courtesy of Marlene Leibold Grothues.)

In 1899, Armin and Max Boehme sold their interest in their ranch to their brother-in-law, Frank Seekatz. Like the Boehmes, the Seekatzes raised cattle in the river valley. Adolph Ihnken (on the left) and Ed Seekatz are pictured building a fence below Milligan Bluff. (Courtesy of the Seekatz family.)

Pictured here in front of their cabin, the Zapata family lived in the river valley and provided for themselves by farming, hunting, and assisting the Seekatz family with their cattle ranch. By 1905, there was talk of a dam being built across the valley. The Zapata homestead would later be flooded after the dam was built and the lake waters rose. (Courtesy of the Seekatz family.)

Cabins like this one were typical for those who lived along the Medina River. The houses were often just one room with no windows and were made of cypress logs or split boards of native wood. An open door provided the only light or air. (Courtesy of the Seekatz family.)

Even before the lake was built, those who lived in the river valley enjoyed the beauty of the rugged landscape. Picnics were a popular pastime and a way to relax with family and friends. This photograph was taken along the area that would become Diversion Lake, below Medina Lake. Rose Ihnken Greener stands next to the family dog. Her husband, Otto, and Adella Seekatz with son Alton in between were successful in climbing a very large boulder. The child to the left of Otto is unidentified. (Courtesy of the Seekatz family.)

Two

A Dream is Born

Henri Castro was the first to see the potential of a dam along the Medina River. Noting the natural formation of the river valley, Castro believed farms could be irrigated if the waters that periodically flooded Box Canyon could be captured. Though an earthen and stone dam was built, Castro knew that one day an even greater dam would be built. Without the means to realize his vision, it remained only a dream. (Courtesy of Leonard Moore.)

It would take almost to the end of the century for another visionary to see the potential that Castro first realized. Around 1894, Alex Walton was hunting in Box Canyon when he observed how the river flowed between the bluffs and how the valley at one point formed a natural basin. Walton sought advice from engineers Terrell Bartlett and Willis Ranney, who responded with enthusiasm. The need for a dam was further highlighted in 1900 when a huge flood swept through the canyon and flooded the Medina Valley below. The waters rose to an estimated 40 feet. This was followed by a 36-foot flood in 1901. The desire to capture these storm waters would gain even more momentum. Above, Walton and Ranney cross the Medina River during their preliminary survey in 1907; below, along with Terrell Bartlett, Clint Kearny, and Thomas Palfrey, they explore Box Canyon.

The young engineers knew they needed capital—and lots of it—in order to undertake such a massive project. They contacted Thomas B. Palfrey, a successful businessman with a talent for raising money. Palfrey got in touch with Clint H. Kearny, who was working on an electric power project in Mexico with Dr. Fred Stark Pearson. Here, Willis Ranney experiences the force of the waters in the Medina River during the preliminary survey in 1907.

Seeing the potential of the project, Dr. Pearson agreed to raise the capital to finance the project. In 1910, he began selling bonds of the San Antonio Land & Irrigation Company to investors in London. Response was so enthusiastic that it was necessary to turn back several investors. Pearson successfully raised $6 million. The Medina Irrigation Company (MICO) was formed to begin acquiring the land necessary to build the dam.

Preparations for the immense construction project began in the spring of 1911. A railroad line would be necessary to bring laborers, materials, and machinery to the job site. The first order of business was to complete negotiations with the Sunset Route of the Southern Pacific Lines to lay tracks from the nearest station at Dunlay to the chosen construction site, a distance of 19 miles.

More than 100 men, mostly from Mexico, were brought in to do the backbreaking job of clearing the land of brush and trees and digging in the hard limestone ground to lay the track and build bridges and trestles. A telephone line was strung between Dunlay and the Medina Irrigation Company offices near the dam site. The work was completed in only 90 days. By August 1911, the railroad was ready to operate.

Attention could now be given to preparing the actual construction site where the dam was to be located. The first order of business was the digging of the foundation. River water was diverted through flumes around the construction site. Mexican and African American laborers worked with nothing more than picks and shovels to remove soil and rock from the riverbed that was carried away by an overhead cable system.

Special attention was given to preparing the bluffs for the construction of the dam and the design of the foundation. The engineers were particularly careful in their specifications for the foundation, not wanting to make the mistakes made in Johnstown, Pennsylvania, where 2,200 lives were lost when a dam failed. The foundation would be 128 feet in width at the base and would extend across the riverbed from one bluff to the other.

DIVRSION
NO. 4 NOV. 27 19[1]

In the harsh landscape of the Texas Hill Country, a dream that was born in the early days of the Texas frontier was becoming a reality. The dream would be realized through imagination and ingenuity and on the backs of thousands of men. The dream harnessed a wilderness and changed thousands more lives through the years—from the farmers who transformed the Medina Valley into rich farmlands to the ranchers who had to adapt to a new landscape and way of life. It was an incredible way to begin the new century.

Three

A DAM IS BUILT

MEDINA VALLEY IRRIG. CO.
JUNE 23, 1913.
MAIN DAM & RESERVOIR

The Medina Dam was a great undertaking and an engineering marvel. International in scope, as Roberto Pachecano of the Medina Lake Preservation Society has pointed out, this great engineering feat took American ingenuity, British capital, and Mexican labor to achieve. A sightseeing brochure from the 1920s describes it: "So stupendous is the conception, so vast the scale of actual accomplishment . . . this everlasting monument to man's mastery over the greatest forces of nature has achieved a deserved fame in the four corners of the earth." (Courtesy of Kristina and Tom Fett.)

On November 10, 1911, construction began on what would be one of the largest dams in the United States. The newly built railroads brought not only building supplies but also many of the workmen and their families to the site. Warehouses and machine shops were built on-site to expedite the project. The massive endeavor was underway.

The dam was designed to be held in place by an edifice sustained by the massive use of solid concrete with very little steel or reinforcing material. A quarry was excavated nearby for the limestone needed to supply crushed rock for the concrete mixture. Barrels of cement made by Texas plants were shipped to Dunlay by rail and then to the mixing plant that was built alongside the construction site.

The cement was mixed together with sand and crushed rock and sent out along the building site by the way of pulleys and lines that crisscrossed over the actual construction. Almost 2,000 barrels a day were required for the construction. By the time the dam was completed, more than 292,000 cubic yards of concrete had been used.

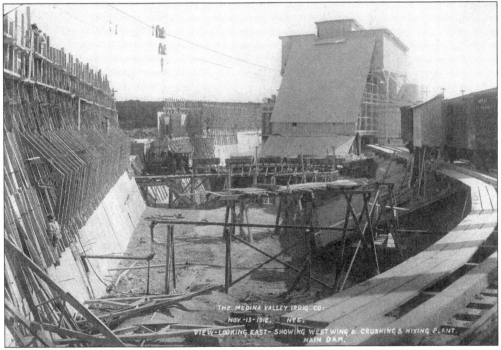

THE MEDINA VALLEY IRRIG. CO.
NOV.-13-1912. No. 6.
VIEW - LOOKING EAST - SHOWING WEST WING & CRUSHING & MIXING PLANT.
MAIN DAM.

When a rainy autumn and winter was forecast for the end of 1912, a sense of urgency took over. The workers were pushed to bring the dam to a sufficient height by the summer of 1912 in order to hold back the autumnal floods that were expected. Crews labored around the clock in two relentless 10-hour shifts, six days a week.

More than 2,000 men were brought in to do the backbreaking, difficult, and often dangerous work on constructing the dam. Everyone was cautioned not to "take any chances of risks that endanger life or limb." The Texas Portland Cement Company issued a card with warnings and guidelines to their employees as a "special and positive caution and notice" that required their signature indicating that they were aware of the potential cost of not being vigilant while on the job. Workers were further instructed to keep the card "in your possession and faithfully follow its instructions . . . that you may aid the Company in avoiding any injury to life and limb by you or your fellow-servant's carelessness." Despite the danger, laborers received $1.25 a day. Skilled workers and carpenters fared a bit better with $2 a day, while foremen received $3 a day.

Work in the quarry was particularly dangerous, due to the use of explosives to blast the limestone. A shed was constructed on-site that quarrymen were instructed to use for protection when blasts were discharged. Because of the nature of the work, anyone reporting to work under the influence of liquor was warned that he would be discharged immediately and arrested for disorderly conduct.

All areas of the construction site were fraught with danger. The cement company warned workers against "crawling through or placing themselves in close proximity to moving belts, shafts, or other gearings, or taking any other unnecessary risks with machinery while in motion." Despite the cautions, it looks as though there was still some room to enjoy a coffee break—even with the extra nicety of a lace tablecloth.

Workers were housed along the banks of the Medina River to be close to the construction site. They lived either in tents or wood-frame barracks. The makeshift village was named Mico, using the acronym for the Medina Irrigation Company. Today, Mico remains a small village of local residents and lakeside businesses.

Of the 1,500 workers, more than 1,300 were brought from Mexico, where they had worked on similar projects for Dr. Fred Pearson's company under the supervision of Clint Kearny. The Mexican workers brought their families with them, and it has been reported that while some lived in tents, others lived in the caves along the river. African Americans and others willing to do heavy manual labor were also hired. (Courtesy of UTSA Libraries Special Collection, Oscar B. Taylor Collection.)

The employee camps became home for the workers and their families. The San Antonio *Light* reported that the camp had electricity, a sewage system, wells to supply water, and a school. The sale of liquor was prohibited, though outsiders were known to come into the camp to sell the workers spirits and other sundry goods. In this photograph, employees' children pose near their living quarters. (Courtesy of UTSA Libraries Special Collection, Oscar B. Taylor Collection.)

While supervisors and managers lived in the relative comfort of wooden cabins, complete with screened-in porches to catch the breeze, the common laborers' accommodations were rough, at best. The semiarid land around the dam site was hot in the summer and could be downright chilly in the winter. Women did their best to provide for their families, including doing laundry in the waters of the Medina River. (Courtesy of Kristina and Tom Fett.)

The camp had its own well-equipped hospital where Dr. John H. Fletcher served as the company's doctor. However, there were deaths due to the dangerous work conditions as well as from diseases. Taken on the boardwalk that ran through the barracks, this photograph shows Dr. Fletcher's wife and Mrs. W.H. Smith with her son Melville on her lap. (Courtesy of UTSA Libraries Special Collection, Oscar B. Taylor Collection.)

The camp became its own little town that strived to be self-sufficient. Claude Gilliam served as constable for the camp as well as the manager of an on-site restaurant, butcher shop, and confectionery. Visitors to the site as well as the employees ate at the restaurant for 50¢ a meal. While most laborers ate meals with their families, payday usually meant a little splurge by eating out. (Courtesy of Kristina and Tom Fett.)

Sundays were a day of rest and play. One could see a motion picture, eat ice cream, or watch the company baseball team play other local teams. Games were played on the flatland along the Medina River. (Courtesy of UTSA's Libraries Special Collection.)

The dam would have lasting ramifications for the families that came here to build it. Many of the Mexican families stayed in the United States, escaping the political unrest of their homeland. Some remained at the lake, while others moved to San Antonio. Natividad Pachecano used the skills he learned to open his own concrete construction business. By the 1960s, the company had 300 employees and specialized in concrete bridges and storm drainage systems. (Courtesy of Roberto Pachecano.)

The construction site became a star attraction for South Texas. Groups of men and women traveled by train and by car to observe firsthand this historic endeavor. Sightseeing expeditions became a lucrative business, luring the curious with promises of all the luxury and comfort one would expect from any first-class tour. Meals were served at the dam site, and women and men would dress in their finery for such a momentous occasion. Above, this crowd arrived from nearby Hondo, Texas, on flatcars to catch the Medina baseball team in action; below, permits were issued to visitors waiving all risks and claims in case of accidents or injuries while at the site. (Above, courtesy of UTSA Libraries Special Collection, Oscar B. Taylor Collection; below, courtesy of Marlene Leibold Grothues.)

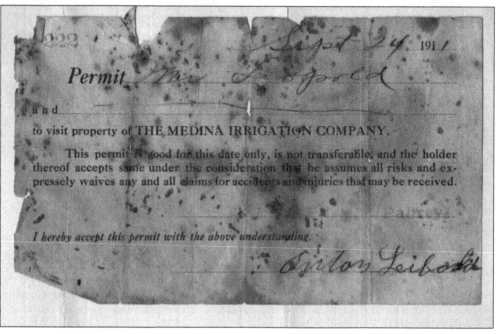

Businesses thrived in the towns and settlements in the vicinity of the dam. The farming community of Rio Medina benefitted while the dam was being built. The Boehme and Haby families established one of the first businesses in the community in the early 1900s. In 1908, Alexander Boehme started a general store and a post office, changing the town's name from San Geronimo to Rio Medina. The town boasted a saloon called the Jockey Club as well as a dance hall, the Mayflower, both owned by Frank Burrell. Frank later sold the Mayflower to Max Boehme in 1913. Both places were a popular destination for the dam's laborers. Above, Joe Geant holds baby Ward Boehme in 1916; below, the Mayflower was said to be built round so the roustabouts could not dance a girl into a corner. (Both images courtesy of Bradford Boehme.)

While construction was going on at the main dam site, the company of Roach, Stanseel, and Crane was awarded the lucrative contract of $850,000 to build the infrastructure that would be necessary for the lake to be used for irrigation. The contract included the excavation of more than 1.4 million cubic yards of earth, the construction of several bridges and culverts, a diversion dam, and two siphons.

Four miles downstream, the smaller Diversion Dam was constructed 50 feet high with a reservoir covering 400 acres when full. Along with a system of canals, Diversion Dam was built to channel water from Medina Lake to be used for irrigation in the farming communities of Medina County, including Castroville, Rio Medina, and Natalia (named for Dr. Pearson's daughter and established and platted during this time by MICO).

By November 1912, the dam was completed. An article in the San Antonio *Light* honored the occasion by observing, "A year ago last July the valley of the Medina River was in the condition left by Nature; now it is blocked by a barrier even larger than the famous Roosevelt Dam in Arizona." The article goes on to note that while the Roosevelt Dam took four years to complete, the Medina Dam took merely a year.

Unfortunately, the lake would take longer to fill behind the dam. As Dr. Pearson reported, "The work was pushed with all possible haste in order that the dam would be of sufficient height in the summer of 1912 to impound the floods which was anticipated . . . but unfortunately the year 1912 proved to be the driest known on record." Dr. Pearson noted that it would take until November 1913 for any water to begin to accumulate behind the dam.

The dam was completed at a cost of about $6 million, raised in England by Dr. Pearson through the sale of bonds. The dam is 1,580 feet long and 164 feet high, with a width of 25 feet at the top and 128 feet at its base. The lake would have 110 miles of shoreline and was built to hold 83 billion gallons of water, or 254,000 acre-feet. Once the rains began, by 1914, limited irrigation had begun to the farms south of the dam. While the primary purpose of the lake was irrigation, the body of water quickly attracted tourists who began to come almost immediately for fishing, swimming, boating, and camping. Above, the first waters to fall over the spillway must have been a welcome sight for the Medina Irrigation Company. At left, Adella Seekatz and her son Alton walk along the top of the newly built Medina Dam. (Above, courtesy of Kristina and Tom Fett; left, courtesy of the Seekatz family.)

Four

A LAKE COMES TO LIFE

After the dam was completed, it took months for Medina Lake to fill. While the engineers and promoters waited impatiently for the rains to come, one can only imagine the reluctance felt by the ranchers and farmers who had lived and worked on the land above the dam. With little wish to leave, they must have dreaded the first heavy rains that fell on the second of October 1913. (Courtesy of the Seekatz family.)

Willie and Ore Branson (left) with her sister and brother-in-law, Victoria and Joe Taylor, traveled four days by automobile to reach San Antonio from East Texas. It was a grand driving tour full of adventure as they camped at night and enjoyed all the sights along the way. Their biggest thrill was to see the newly constructed Medina Dam. Arriving before the lake filled, they were able to pose at the base of the dam. The family fell in love with the Texas Hill Country, and several of their descendants live at Medina Lake today. (Both images courtesy of Darrell Revet, Darlene Revet Croft, and the Revet family.)

The water steadily rose over the first year and a half, and by 1914 there was 125 feet of water behind the Medina Dam, ready to carry water to the farms below. At the last minute, several homes were hastily moved up the hills, where they barely escaped a watery grave. As ranchers above the dam scrambled to secure a new way of life, farmers below the dam planted their crops in anticipation of the water that would be available for irrigation. Tourists arrived even faster than the rains, eager to enjoy the natural beauty of the lake. (Both images courtesy of the Seekatz family.)

Edward Asa Johnson Sr. came from Oklahoma to see the Medina Dam being built in 1911. He liked the wild and wooly country and moved his family near Kerrville before settling along the lake. Here, Edward Asa poses with his family next to the wagon that brought them to Texas with the venison that would be served for Christmas dinner. (Courtesy of Burgin and Valli Johnson.)

Edward Asa's son Edward Johnson was the principal at Pipe Creek School prior to leasing Goat Hill Camp from Theresa Spettle. His daughter Loy Ed Johnson Alanis sits on her father's lap at Goat Hill Camp, where the family lived in the old Spettle House, one of the homes that almost did not make it out of the lake bottom before the lake filled. (Courtesy of Loy Ed Johnson Alanis.)

The Johnsons bought the fishing camp Goat Hill and rented boats to the tourists who brought their personal motors from town. Daughter Loy Ed counted out the minnows and took care of the money while her brother Bujrgin tied the boats to the dock. The family ran the camp until 2007. (Courtesy of Loy Ed Johnson Alanis.)

Anton Leibold's father, John, originally established the family's ranch along the Medina River. By 1914, a good portion of the ranch lay under the waters of the lake. Needing to diversify his livelihood, Anton opened the first fishing camp on the new lake. While he continued to ranch on higher ground, the fishing camp proved to be very successful. Here, Anton (center) serves as a fishing guide. (Courtesy of Marlene Leibold Grothues.)

Anton and his wife, Annie, took in boarders for duck hunting, fishing, and camping. Along with his son Milton, Anton built cabins and a bunkhouse to accommodate their guests as well as fishing boats to rent and fancier excursion boats for sightseers to view the lake. The view of the dam farther down the lake was popular with guests. (Courtesy of Marlene Leibold Grothues.)

The Leibolds became well known for their accommodations and received guests from all over Texas. Annie sold staples such as eggs, butter, and milk to the campers, and Anton was trusted to care for the outboard motors of his wealthier clients. Often, clients would write and give permission for Anton to allow a friend to borrow the motor while at the lake. These rather well-dressed men enjoy an excursion with one of Anton's workers. (Courtesy of Marlene Leibold Grothues.)

The fishing camp and lake became popular with soldiers from the military bases in nearby San Antonio. Seen here with Anton (left) is Sergeant Croft, an Army soldier from Fort Sam Houston. Croft began spending his leave with the Leibolds and soon became a family fixture. After he left the Army, he moved into one of the small cabins. (Courtesy of Marlene Leibold Grothues.)

The old bunkhouse and cabins still stand, and the family continues to serve vacationers on the site of the old fishing camp with their Medina Lake RV Park. Many of their guests have been coming to the camp and renting the cabins for four generations. (Courtesy of Marlene Leibold Grothues.)

The Seekatz ranching family fought hard to keep their lands from being condemned and inundated by the waters held back by Medina Dam. Sitting next to their new home that overlooked the lake, Lorraine Chandler and Adella Seekatz must have felt a mixture of awe and bewilderment as their ranching way of life gave way to tourists with their newfangled automobiles and motorboats back in 1916. (Courtesy of the Seekatz family.)

The Seekatz family leased their new shoreline along Lake Medina, which was developed into a successful resort business replete with hotels, boat leasing, and guided fishing tours. Adella Seekatz is pictured here with a customer in front of the E.H. Seekatz Store, which she filled with groceries and fishing supplies, and provided gasoline for locals and tourists alike. She proudly advertised sandwiches, light lunches, and free tables. (Courtesy of the Seekatz family.)

In 1928, Frank Seekatz stands in front of the rock pillars that still mark the entrance to Seekatz Park. The Seekatz family leased property to families who wanted a little getaway on the Lake Medina waterfront. Families spent many a summer holiday driving up the rugged hill-country roads to build their weekend cabins and fishing docks. Over the past nine decades, generations have enjoyed happy summer days and tall fishing tales mixed with memories of long dusty rides back to San Antonio on rough gravel roads. Ed Seekatz traveled those same long roads to pick up ice in San Antonio at the Lone Star Ice Company to ice down the catch of the day. (Both images courtesy of the Seekatz family.)

At Camp Medina, the Seekatz family leased their land to new tourist-friendly establishments such as the Wilson Lodge. The cove offered spectacular views of Lake Medina and the surrounding hills, as well as shelter for myriad fishing and touring boats. Rough roads made overnight stays a necessity in the early days, and the lodge keepers tempted their overnight guests for even longer

stays by providing the best in dining, accommodations, and entertainment. This photograph shows Wilson Lodge overlooking the cove. A line of fishing boats is strung together waiting for guests to rent them for a day. (Courtesy of the Seekatz family.)

Wilson Lodge at Camp Medina provided overnight accommodations at a rustic yet comfortable getaway from the city. The lodge was constructed of local hill country materials, including limestone rocks and cedar. A huge fireplace added a comforting glow to the wooden dance floor and heavy beamed ceilings. Laughter kept time to the two-step as anglers became hoofers dancing to the upright piano on Saturday nights. Sadly, an errant spark from an evening fire may have caused the lodge's demise to fire. Without a fire department to save the day, there was little anyone could do but watch in dismay. (Both images courtesy of the Seekatz family.)

Harold Zinsmeister's father and other local craftsmen built fishing boats for the camps. The crafts were constructed of local cypress, known for its strength and durability in water. Fisherman and families would rent the boats and guides would pull them in a line behind a motorboat, dropping them off one by one at their favorite fishing holes. No one remembers whether there was a set time for the guide to return, but local knowledge has it that everyone made it back to camp for the fish fry. Below, guests at the Felthouse family's house on Angel Drive stand in front of their homemade boat. (Above, courtesy of the Seekatz family; below, courtesy of Gary Cox.)

Call Gate (medina Lake)

To expedite trips to the lake, toll roads were built by San Antonio businessmen to replace the rough roads leading to the lake. Many fishermen resented the toll and would go around the gate without paying. The tollhouse still standing on FM 1283 is a reminder of an organ-grinding monkey in a red cap who made collecting the 50¢ easier from excited children. Nothing remains of the tollbooth on the old Park Road. (Courtesy of the Witte Museum, San Antonio, Texas.)

Contractor Martin Wright built a luxury log cabin on the high bluffs overlooking the lake. Along with other San Antonio businessmen, Wright actively sought investors to help develop the Southern Club during the 1920s. Along with well-appointed cabins, a three-story native rock clubhouse would cater to wealthy patrons by providing the finest in lakeside accommodations. The club was an unrealized dream, perhaps a casualty of the Great Depression. (Courtesy of the Witte Museum, San Antonio, Texas.)

Joe Granieri was instrumental in the development of the lake's resort business, opening Hotel Granieri in Mico as well as a hotel and tavern on the road to the dam. After his divorce, he opened a tavern, boat launch, grocery store, and weekend cabins on the waterfront. Competition for tourists was fierce, so Granieri and his neighbor Frank Seekatz built their own roads to cleverly direct traffic to their businesses. (Courtesy of Chris and Debbie Heyen.)

An Italian immigrant, Joe Granieri came to the area when he drove a taxi shuttle to and from the Medina Dam construction site. He is seen here in his pride and joy, *The Ghost*, an early motorboat. Evinrude put out its first gasoline motor in 1909, and by the time Medina Lake was full the new sound of whirling motors began to fill the coves. Speedboat races would later pull in throngs of tourists. (Courtesy of Chris and Debbie Heyen.)

As the roads improved, wealthy families began to buy property and build fine homes on the banks of the lake to escape the heat and scurry of San Antonio. Families could spend vacation time together and enjoy the finer things of life amidst the beauty and tranquility of the waterfront. Above, Horace and Mary Lee Masterson play in front of the Masterson weekend home on Masterson Point. Below, the Masterson family is seen enjoying their custom wooden pleasure boat on Medina Lake in 1924. (Courtesy of UTSA Special Libraries, Beatrice Masterson Richards Collection.)

San Antonio families constructed their weekend homes not only to get away from the city, but also as a place to gather friends and entertain. Most homes were built like the Fred and Elsie Felthouse home with the abundant cedar trees and rock found on the property. Homes included massive fireplaces for the winter and screened-in sleeping porches for the summer. (Courtesy of Gary Cox.)

Entertainment at the lake was not limited to water sports. Hunting was another favorite pastime. Fred and Elsie Felthouse are pictured here with friends in front of their Angel Cove house. The large bag of trophy deer and wild turkeys was enough for a feast. (Courtesy of Gary Cox.)

The roads to Medina Lake were rough and dusty, as photographed here on the corner of Park Road 37 and FM 1283. Signs advertise Coca-Cola, Adolph's Place, and Whitley's Place. Adolph's was owned by the Mazurek family, who provided a stop on the way to the lake to fill up on groceries, ice, and cold drinks. It was also a neighborhood gathering place. (Courtesy of Rena and Adolph Mazurek Jr.)

Adolph and Irene Mazurek also ran the corner filling station since the 1930s. They expanded the business through the years to include an icehouse and lumberyard. In 1960, they opened a kitchen and added a restaurant to the business. Today, Adolph's Restaurant continues to serve the best steaks and burgers in the county. (Courtesy of Rena and Adolph Mazurek Jr.)

Roads began to improve on the upper lake, thanks in part to Avalon Ranch developer Lester Whipple, who donated acreage to the state for a park in order to justify the Angler's Club's push for a state-funded highway. Local businesses prospered as more people came not only for weekends but also for their permanent homes. Avalon Grocery and Café was located on newly built Park Road 37. (Courtesy of Ruth Tschirhart.)

Another social spot for the residents of Medina Lake was the Medina Lake School. This land in Mico was donated by Frank Seekatz in 1922, and the structure remained in operation as a school and a meeting place until after World War II. It is seen here during a very rare snowstorm. Today, all that remains is the foundation's concrete slab. (Courtesy of Chris and Debbie Heyen.)

Frank Seekatz also donated land in Mico for the construction of St. Francis Chapel. Many community fundraisers were held and supported by all denominations to raise the money to construct the building. The chapel became a fisherman's worship destination, with the local marinas ferrying families of all faiths to the tiny chapel overlooking Medina Lake. (Courtesy of the Seekatz family.)

Apparently, there was no fanfare at the time construction of the Medina Dam was completed in just one year. Rev. Cyril Matthew Kuehne, SM, pastor of St. Francis Chapel and the author of *Ripples from Medina Lake*, corrected this oversight when he held a ceremony to bless the dam in 1942. (Courtesy of Doug King.)

56

Five

A COMMUNITY GROWS

During World War II, President Roosevelt encouraged outdoor recreation to keep up morale. Following the war, roads were improved, the workweek was reduced to five days, and there was more leisure time to enjoy. The booming 1960s saw a surge in lakeside development, including a new post office. A contest was held, and winner Dixie Hammonds named the unincorporated upper lake Lakehills. (Courtesy of Kristina and Tom Fett.)

New businesses developed in Lakehills to support the increase in tourists and new residents. As the community grew, the churches came not only to serve the religious needs of the people but also to function as social gathering places. Established in 1956 at the old Rock Store on Park Road 37, St. Victor's Chapel was one of the first. St. Victor's has continued to grow since then and is known for its annual flea market and barbecue. (Courtesy of Ruth Tschirhart.)

On June 14, 1959, the first church service for the Methodist church was held in a tent on Robert A. Zigler's property on Eighth Street in Lakehills. A heavy rainstorm caused the tent to sag so that it had to be restretched, and mud damage to the chairs meant they had to be cleaned. Zigler donated the property, and the congregation built the Lakehills United Methodist Church. Today, the church has outreach programs including a community garden, a food pantry, a Wesley nurse, and annual fish-fry fundraisers. (Courtesy of Lakehills United Methodist Church.)

In April 1962, a new church was conceived and built in Lakehills and was named the Park Road 37 Baptist Church. In 1979, the board voted to drop their affiliation with the Southern Baptist Church and change the name to the Faith Chapel of Lakehills. Today, the location is known as the Lighthouse Church of Lakehills (pictured above). A 30-foot-tall structure lights the way for their services, held every Sunday. The Lakehills Baptist Church (pictured below) is now a thriving church located on FM 1283 and high on the hill next door to the Bandera County Annex. (Both images courtesy of Karen Downing Ripley.)

While many establishments would come and go, Joe's Place and Red Cove (bought by Joe Granerie in 1947) remained as stalwart examples of a dream that does not die easily. When Joe Granerie retired in 1978, Joe's Place was leased to Lackland Air Force Base as a recreation camp for active duty and retired military and Department of Defense employees. When the lease was up, the family resumed the business and continued the long tradition of providing access to Lake Medina with a launch, marina, and recreational facilities. The children pictured at left are rowing boats at Joe's Place; below is Red Cove's distinctive sign. (Left, courtesy of Chris and Debbie Heyen; below, courtesy of the Medina Lake Volunteer Fire Department.)

On October 16, 1961, a group of 42 citizens met to organize the Medina Lake Volunteer Fire Department. Real estate developer Lester Whipple donated land on Park Road 37 for the site. Funds were raised, and the first cement truck began work on the building in August 1962. The community continues to rely on the volunteer fire department to provide fire protection and some of the best brisket and barbecue in the state. (Courtesy of Kristina and Tom Fett.)

The Mico Volunteer Fire Department was established around 1960 on land donated by Alton and Lema Seekatz. Not only did the MVFD set out to fight fires, but it also provided a gathering place where neighbors could work together toward common goals. "It was a turning point; we had a place for people to meet," said one longtime resident. "And, since there weren't many volunteers, we women learned to drive the fire truck as well." (Courtesy of Mico Volunteer Fire Department.)

The state park at Medina Lake provided easy access to the lake for boaters, water-lovers, and fisherman. Pictured above, a grand, opening-day dedication of the park was held. Day-trippers came in droves to the new boat launch, restrooms, and floating docks. The state eventually turned the park over to Bandera County, which now maintains and oversees the facility. Developer Lester Whipple donated land for the state park in order to justify the private Angler's Club's push for a state highway leading to Medina Lake. Unfortunately, Park Road 37 cut a swath through many waterfront properties, such as Whitley's lakeside resort, pictured below, next to the park road. Sadly, the dangerous turns of the road took an even greater toll when August Whitley missed negotiating the treacherous dead man's curve above Schott's Ranch and lost his life on the road. (Above, courtesy of Kristina and Tom Fett; below, courtesy of Karen Downing Ripley.)

New marinas began springing up as the new roads made travel to the lake a one-day affair. Pictured above, Rudes was established at the old Whitley building. The site was later occupied by Lakeside, pictured below. They provided a marina, cabins, restaurant, and dances on the weekends. The windows were open, and the southerly breezes blew continually. If a person docked and had no shirt or shoes, he went to the Chick Shack for sandwiches and sodas. If he had a shirt and shoes, he could walk across Park Road 37 for a home-cooked meal and stay for the dance and a beer. (Above, courtesy of Glen Sescila; below, courtesy of Karen Downing Ripley.)

New businesses developed along Park Road 37 toward the state park. Beyond Rudes was Bob's Cove, which offered a covered marina, dance pavilion, showers, and a convenience store. Guests brought their campers and left them until their next visit. Owner Bob Lehman, a Southwestern Bell Telephone employee, decided that if everyone was going to stay they might as well pay for the upkeep. Bob's son Ralph and wife, Ann, continued leasing to many of the same families who for decades built docks and cabanas to enjoy their little weekend community. Bob's Cove was closed to the public when sold to a California executive in the early 2000s. Above, a roadside sign advertises Rudes; below, this fisherman has caught a big one at Bob's Cove. (Above, courtesy of Ruth Tschirhart; below, courtesy of Ralph Lehman.)

Bob's Cove served as Mariner Girl Scout Troop 81's moorage for its 16-foot sailboat, the *Jean Lafitte*. The Mariners were a unique troop whose special emphasis was on sailing. Their leader, Camilla Campbell, was a children's history author who enjoyed teaching her Girl Scouts entrepreneurial skills by helping them set up their own corporation to support their sailing activities. Before setting sail from Bob's Cove, the girls had to swim out to a floating metal drum and untie and swim the boat to shore, where it could be rigged to sail. Karen Ripley remembers diving into the water in March and having her heart stop from the cold. But the excitement of sailing down the lake to Red Cove for burgers got it pumping again. (Both images courtesy of Karen Downing Ripley.)

On the Mico side of Medina Lake, Joe's Place continued operation, while other establishments were bought and resold. New businesses flourished when the lake was full and then would fail when the rains did not come. Profits rose or fell with the level of the lake. Red Cove was located just before Joe's Place, and the Granieri heirs continued to run both establishments into the 2000s. (Courtesy of Chris and Debbie Heyen.)

Lakehills had more available land to develop and easier access to the water than nearby Mico. Enterprising couples came to the lake and established businesses, including Cousins Point at the end of George's Road. Through drought and flood, owners Bill and Betty Yunc were devoted to clearing land, planting shade trees, and building shelters, ramps, and docks, as well as promoting special events to appeal to the tourist trade. (Courtesy of Kim and Alena Yunc.)

Pebble Beach was platted in the 1960s by Kent Baltzell and Jake Webb as a planned community built on a peninsula. It has a rich history as the jumping-off point where adventurers and gamblers would ferry across to Tiki Island to play poker out of reach of the local authorities. Landowners gambled on their new subdivision by banding together to pave roads and upgrade water systems using hard work and ingenuity. (Courtesy of Karen Downing Ripley.)

Tiki Island continues to sit as a sentinel guarding the waters of Medina Lake. It has had many owners and names through the years and has been reported to have been a speakeasy, a gambling house, and even a resort with a South Pacific theme. Tiki Island looks like a Grecian isle when the water is low, looks forlorn when flooded, and looks like home when one is swimming toward it. (Courtesy of Ron Bird.)

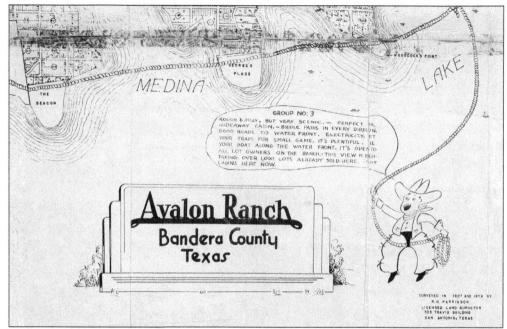

Avalon Ranch was developed by Lester Whipple, who promoted the upper lake as a wonderful and affordable place to get away from the city. For $25, families could purchase a 25-by-90-foot lot. Advertisements enticed potential buyers by bragging about the excellent fishing. As one poster proclaimed, "Catfish as large as 80 lbs. have been caught in Medina Lake." Families would pack up on Friday afternoons and drive out to their lots. Cedar was cleared, and the men would pitch in and build shelters while the women cooked and the kids played. Around the lake, makeshift cabins have been remodeled dozens of times and heirs continue to meet at the lake for fun in the sun. Above is a detail from an Avalon sales poster. Below, Avalon's Elmhurst Point juts into Elm Cove across from Pebble Beach. (Both images courtesy of Kristina and Tom Fett.)

Perhaps much of Medina Lake's magic comes from its unusual dragon shape. When the lake was formed, hills became islands and valleys became coves as the Medina River wrapped its way toward the Gulf of Mexico in the sinuous shape of a fiery dragon. This image inspired the name Avalon, after the mythical island where the famous sword Excalibur was forged. (Courtesy of Kristina and Tom Fett.)

Longtime lake resident Panchita Thomson sold real estate for Lake Medina Properties well into her nineties. As a child, she watched the dam being built, and her community spirit won the hearts of many as she helped strangers become residents. Real estate professionals including Dan Alanis, Wilbur and Olga Bradford, Ronnie Basinger, Lou Holiday, Mike Mallory, and Karen Ripley followed in Thomson's footsteps to become local leaders and give back to the community. (Courtesy of Kristina and Tom Fett.)

Cedar Rock

BANDERA COUNTY
TEXAS

In the 1950s, Fred F. Morgan, a successful Corpus Christi businessman, bought Cedar Rock, the estate of a Houston oil tycoon located at the end of Breezy Point. Morgan became a successful Bandera County developer, establishing Morgan Heights and other businesses and properties. He lived out his days at Cedar Rock, a six-acre estate replete with tennis courts, a walk-in deep freeze, and wine vault. Built of indigenous material, its massive rock walls and exposed cedar rafters and trim are striking. The estate was purchased and remodeled by Don and Sharon Sloan in 2005. The Sloans continue to entertain on the breezy, oak-shaded lawn that spills down to the lake opposite the cliffs of Mormon's Bluff. Fred Morgan is pictured below on his horse, Chief. (Both images courtesy of Don and Sharon Sloan.)

Another famous businessman, Harry Jersig, bought and developed a piece of land down the lane from Cedar Rock that he called Star Lot, after his Lone Star brewery. It was a modern design with a sweeping unsupported concrete staircase leading to entertainment rooms overlooking Medina Lake on Echo Point. Jersig entertained the rich and famous at Star Lot until the 1970s, when he donated the facility to the Girl Scouts. In the 1990s, Doug and Helen Frank bought and remodeled Star Lot as their home. The echoes of decades of fun continue to be heard as the Franks hold community events and fundraisers that include the annual Boys and Girls Club's Casino Night. Star Lot is pictured above. Below, Harry Jersig promoted Lone Star beer at the lake by placing advertisements on tourist maps and brochures. (Above, courtesy of Karen Downing Ripley; below, courtesy of the Frontier Times Museum.)

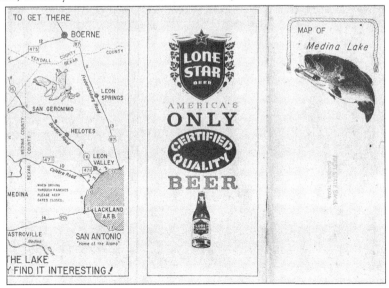

Turk's store started as Mr. Ink's real estate office back in the 1940s until the Neal family turned it into a Red & White Grocery store. In 1957, Lin Toerck purchased the store and named it Turk's Grocery. His brother Ervin made the little corner grocery a hub of the community where old-timers would gather for their mail. When the Toercks retired in 1977, they sold the business to Gene and Barbara Ott, who converted the store's small storage area into a saloon where anglers would show off their catch. Turk's changed hands many more times and was purchased by Gwen Smith in 2008 to become a sandwich shop where the local Writers of the Lake met and spun yarns. Across George's Road, Paradise Boats and D&H Auto provide automobile and boat service and repairs. For over 20 years, the only thing brighter than the August sun has been Doris's welcoming grin as she pushes her little stool up to your car and gives you full service with a smile. (Above, courtesy of Jane Swager Perkins; below, courtesy of Karen Downing Ripley.)

Time changes along the lake as older businesses close or change ownership. Fred's Dam Place changed ownership from Fred Christillus to become Cedar Point and then Bedrock Resort, owned by Steve and Roxanne Balik-Bonahoom. Newer businesses have capitalized on sports trends. Former Sea World performers Mike and Shirlee Crandall established Wally's Water Sports in 2001 next to Rural Murray's Old Mico Inn. Specializing in trick skiing, they offer both the equipment and the training. (Courtesy of Mike and Shirlee Crandall.)

A motocross course on FM 1283 between Mico and Lakehills was established in 2001 to train world-class competitors including Heath Voss, winner of the 2004 World Super Cross Title. In 2010, Voss established Hangar 13, offering helicopter tours over the lake. (Courtesy of Heath Voss.)

As Lakehills grew, businesses developed to serve the residents. Dusti's became the local grocery store on Park Road 37 that served locals for over 25 years. The store was under construction during the great snow of 1984 when the Heidelbergs had to heat up the interior to melt the snow and save the building's roof from crashing down under the weight. In the foreground, granddaughter Dusti races toward the camera with her ribbon. (Courtesy of Esther Heidelberg.)

Gordon Nordlund's Viking Shopping Center on Park Road 37 was the prime location for many businesses and the Lakehills Post Office. Nordlund was active in community affairs and a strong supporter of the Boy Scouts. When the post office was closed in the late 1990s, development slowed down along Park Road 37. (Courtesy of Gordon Nordlund.)

Kenneth and Linda Ritchie bought their liquor store from Gordon Nordlund and rented space at his Viking Shopping Center for the first few years. In 2000, they moved J.R.'s Liquors to FM 1283. Business really picked up when Linda painted the building like a red barn with white trim. It was Joe who said, "Let's paint it red, white, *and* blue and put the Texas flag on the roof!" (Courtesy of Kenneth and Linda Ritchie.)

The Avalon Store and Café was located on Park Road 37 under a grove of huge oak trees. The restaurant has had many owners and was at one time a coffee shop. In 2002, Bobby Harris and his wife, Patty, opened Tadpole's in the old café. Bobby Harris served as county commissioner and was instrumental in upgrading roads, trash disposal, and the county park. (Courtesy of Bobby and Patty Harris.)

Robert and Jane Swager bought Pop's Place in 1972 as a place for local fishermen and tourists to launch their boats and purchase beer and supplies. Jane's mother, Mildred Anderson, ran Pop's until 1978, when the flood destroyed most of the structures. Robert and Jane then purchased 10 acres on Park Road 37 with the plan of building a home. While clearing the property, they acquired a large number of cedar logs and large rocks. After setting up two mobile homes on the property, Robert built a small cabin that he called Jane's Log Cabin. Jane soon filled the cabin with handcrafts that she, Mildred, and other local women made and sold on consignment. (Both images courtesy of Jane Swager Perkins.)

Tom and Virginia Gibson moved to Medina Lake in the 1970s and began buying up foreclosed lake properties on the Bandera County Courthouse steps. In addition to promoting land sales in Lake Medina Highlands, they also created Clegg's RV Park, where patrons could rent space on the shores of Medina Lake to park campers, launch boats, and enjoy fishing from the dock. (Courtesy of Willy Vorhes.)

Kelly Ranson and the Laurel Creek Joint Venture donated land to the Lakehills Courthouse Annex, which was constructed in 1996 on FM 1283. Dan C. Alanis III, county commissioner; Ernest C. Reich III, constable; James MacMillan, sheriff; and Bobbie Jo Basinger, justice of the peace, served on the building committee. Residents no longer have to drive to the county seat of Bandera every time an issue arises. (Courtesy of Karen Downing Ripley.)

The Medina Lake Betterment Association (MLBA) was initially established to address concerns by property owners that the lake's water was being mismanaged by the BMA Water District. The association expanded its objectives to build a civic center and improve the quality of life for the community. As the years progressed, each generation added its gifts and talents to the MLBA—especially Bob Caswell and Barbara Engel. Bob drew from his Cajun background in New Orleans, and Barbara lent her business savvy as the owner of Cutaway Salon to create the first Medina Lake Cajun Festival in 1995 as a fundraiser for the association. The festival has become a highlight drawing Cajun fans to Lakehills each year. Above, Cajun music adds to the atmosphere of the festivities; below, Barbara Engel and Bob Caswell are seen manning the Cajun Food booth. (Both images courtesy of Bob Caswell and Barbara Engel.)

B.G. Watson's Medina Lake Country Club has been a favorite local watering hole at Lakehills for decades. B.G. has loyal customers and staff members who treat each other like family. Another community supporter is the American Legion Post 410, which received its charter in 1967. Members collect donations each year by giving out paper poppies symbolizing the red poppy of Flanders fields in memory of the fallen in World War I and all subsequent wars involving American soldiers. The annual Lakehills Fourth of July parade is also sponsored by the American Legion. American flags line the way as the parade winds its way up Park Road 37. Above, from left to right, Bob Stevens, Wayne Saunders, Horseshoe Charlie Williams, and Darryl Lambert celebrate the Fourth of July parade at the country club. Below, American Legion member Ron Bird adds flair and color to the parade. (Above, courtesy of B.G. Watson; below, courtesy of Ron Bird.)

The ground-breaking ceremony for the Lakehills Library was held in 2002. The library offers story time for children, books to check out for all ages, used book sales, genealogy, computer access, and modern facilities for community meetings. Loyal volunteers and staff members provide literacy programs to residents of the Lakehills area. The land was donated by Eddie Leibold. The Leibolds also donated land for the Leibold Sports Complex. Supported by an army of volunteers, the complex encourages children of all ages to get out and play ball. Pictured at the ground-breaking ceremony are, from left to right, Eddie Leibold, Loy Ed Alanis, Olga Bradford, Judge Richard Evans, and Cormer County commissioner Ronnie Basinger. (Left, courtesy of Lakehills Library; below, courtesy of Karen Downing Ripley.)

Hill Country Elementary serves around 500 students and earned a "recognized" rating by the State of Texas in 2011 for excellence in education. The facility serves the children in the community by hosting after-school programs that include the Girl Scouts and the Boys and Girls Club. (Courtesy of Karen Downing Ripley.)

Jaime and Michelle Rodriguez opened La Cabana Mexican Restaurant as a family operation in the mid-1990s on FM 1283 in the heart of Lakehills. After consistently serving up the best Tex-Mex in the county, they outgrew their first little restaurant and moved up the road to a larger facility. They continue to serve traditional Mexican-food favorites to order—and with a smile. (Courtesy of Karen Downing Ripley.)

In the spirit of the original settlers of Medina Lake, June Reedy and her husband, Tom, left their executive life behind and, in their seventies, set out to turn 200 acres of Lakehills into a working cattle and goat ranch. Amid trials and tribulations, they succeeded not only in goat-herding skills and cattle ranching but also in creating their home atop the area's highest hill with a breathtaking view of Medina Lake resplendent in sunrise and in sunset. (Courtesy of Tom and June Reedy.)

Sandee Bowman is pictured in front of her "free roaming" cattery, founded in 2007 to provide luxury sanctuary for kitties longing for adoption. Sandee and her volunteers place 800 to 1,000 kitties a year into qualified homes by reference, as well as through adoption events at PetSmart. Linda Jacobson of Lakehills Art Gallery created the wonderful painting of the Best Little Cat House in Texas. (Courtesy of Sandee Bowman.)

Daisy Scouts learn the art of selling Girl Scout cookies on the corner of Park Road 37 and FM 1283. The South Texas Girl Scouts hold an annual sailing camp at Adrienne King's Medina Lake house at Goat Hill each summer. The girls pitch their tents and leave their makeup and cell phones behind. The Girls Scouts of America share a special bond with Medina Lake, as both celebrate their centennials in 2012. (Courtesy of Karen Downing Ripley.)

Older girls still just want to have fun, too. The Damsels are an informal group of women who live around Medina Lake. They get together to share food and friends. Members are pictured here during a 2010 style show that was organized by local theater director Ann Young at Helen Frank's home on Breezy Point. The Damsels modeled clothes from local boutiques that were for sale following the show. (Courtesy of Karen Downing Ripley.)

Far away from the hustle and bustle of the city, family friends Delbert Downing and Stacy Saunders enjoy the good life under the cedars at Medina Lake. There has never been a better place to bring friends and family, young and old, together. (Courtesy of Wayne Saunders.)

As the sun goes down on Medina Lake, the mermaid at Ann and John Dale's home high above Friendly Point gazes longingly as the sailboat below sails toward a bright new day. (Courtesy of John and Ann Dale.)

Six

WET AND DRY, NATURE'S WRATH

Medina Lake is not a constant-level lake. Always at the mercy of nature, the lake's water level has fluctuated depending upon whether heavy rains arrive or if the rains fail to come at all. For those who rely on the lake for their livelihood and homes, weather extremes can mean the difference between prosperity or loss. (Courtesy of the Seekatz family.)

In 1900 and 1901, flash flooding in the area led the developers of the dam to be optimistic about having sufficient rainfall after the dam was completed to adequately fill the reservoir for irrigation use. Unfortunately, the first year after the dam was completed proved to be drier than usual. The lake did not fill until 1914. (Courtesy of the Bexar-Medina-Atascosa Water District.)

The 1920s showed relatively stable water levels, but by the mid-1930s the rain had come, and by 1936 water was flowing over the dam's spillway. The wet/dry cycles of South Texas are caused mainly by the fluctuations in the Pacific Ocean's water temperatures. If the water temperature rises, the rain increases, and a drop in the temperature will cause the rain to decrease. Here, water falls over Diversion Dam during a rainy season. (Courtesy of the Seekatz family.)

Through the years, Camp Medina experienced both high and low water. The 1936 flood inundated the camp where rising water came just inches from many of its buildings. The camp's drink stand remained high and dry, but the garage was not so lucky. As quickly as the water rose, it receded. Medina Lake acts like a bathtub, filling up quickly during a flood and then lowering slowly as if someone has pulled out the stopper. During this flood, damage was minimal, with only mud and debris to clean up after the waters fell. (Both images courtesy of the Seekatz family.)

Following World War II, the rain had stopped and the lake dramatically receded. Adella Seekatz drove to Camp Medina and discovered that the Seekatz boathouse and dock were no longer sitting on the water but were well up on the bank. In the photograph, a boat has been beached on the shore as well. (Courtesy of the Seekatz family.)

By the late 1940s, lake levels began to drop as the early stages of a devastating drought began to take effect. The trunks of oak, pecan, and cypress trees remain below the surface of the lake. This 1948 photograph taken at Camp Medina shows that the water levels were low enough for these ancient trees to be visible. Residents still tie bottles to the limbs to warn boaters about hidden dangers. (Courtesy of the Seekatz family.)

As the water levels dropped, fishermen began to catch the less desirable predator fish, the gar. Gars are primitive fish, heavily armored with tough scales, and have long jaws filled with long, sharp teeth. They feed on smaller fish and are extremely hardy, able to tolerate conditions that would kill most other fish. When water levels are low, they can periodically come to the surface to take a gulp of air as oxygen levels in the water decrease. (Courtesy of the Seekatz family.)

By the 1950s, the drought had become the most devastating on record, characterized by both low rainfall and extremely high temperature. In 1956, a widespread effort by the San Antonio Anglers Club to eliminate the overpopulated gar began. There was a planned fish kill during which all the fish in the lake were poisoned. To repopulate the lake with trophy white and black bass, the Anglers Club established a fish hatchery at the lake. (Courtesy of the Seekatz family.)

The lake essentially disappeared during the drought of the 1950s, and the resiliency of the lake's residents was called upon once again. Residents such as the Leibold and Johnson families began farming the fertile soil of the lakebed. Milton Leibold grew grain to feed chickens and hogs and hay for cattle. Even spinach was grown commercially. Milton's daughter Marlene recalls learning to drive on the lake bottom where "there wasn't anything to run into." (Courtesy of Marlene Leibold Grothues.)

Whenever the lake level decreases, a new dramatic landscape is revealed where limestone bluffs and the original riverbed are visible once more. The majesty of the dam is uncovered as the sheer, monolithic wall of concrete is exposed. Water management problems are exacerbated as the needs of lake residents conflict with those of the people living downstream who rely on the water for irrigation. (Courtesy of the Seekatz family.)

90

The rains began to fall again by the late 1950s, and the area went into a relatively normal cycle of wet and dry until 1978. In August 1978, the usually calm Medina River surged as a result of rainwater from Tropical Storm Amelia. The storm stalled over the Hill Country and dumped up to 20 inches of rain. The river rose to 45 feet—35 feet above the river's normal 10 feet. As the raging wall of water moved downstream, residents of Medina Lake could only wait for it to hit. On the back of the above photograph is written, "When the big waves first started." As the flood hit, the waters rose rapidly and washed away homes, buildings, and docks. The devastation was described as the worst the area had seen since the flood of 1900. (Both images courtesy of Jane Swager Perkins.)

The cycle of drought and flooding began again in 1996, when the state declared a drought disaster, the second worst since the 1950s. Because of the drought and an increased demand for irrigation water, Medina Lake dropped 26 feet below the dam's spillway. In 1998, the area saw significant flooding, but in 2002 a flood of record proportion hit when almost a year's worth of rainfall fell between June 27 and July 5. The Medina River was turned into what the *Bandera Bulletin* called "a raging liquid holocaust." The force of the 12-foot-deep water crashing over the spillway was so great that there were concerns that the almost 100-year-old dam could give way. The lake rose to within inches of the top of the dam. This could have weakened the dam's structural integrity if water had gone over the top. (Both images courtesy of Robert and Barbara Brischetto.)

In 2002, the waters of Medina Lake rose to the highest level since the lake was created. Extensive damage was done to houses that survived with little to no damage from either the 1978 or 1998 flood. It was estimated that 40 to 50 homes in Lakehills were destroyed and 75 to 80 were severely damaged, as were many more in the Wharton Dock's area. Looting became a problem, and Sheriff James MacMillan closed the lake to watercraft. He told the *Bandera Bulletin*, "People were driving boats through people's yards and around their houses. That was causing wave damage. Also we want to give property owners the first chance to recover missing items before someone else does." Pictured above, many lost their docks and personal watercraft as they floated into the lake. Tiki Island's flooded cabins are pictured below. (Both images courtesy of Robert and Barbara Brischetto.)

On July 5, 2002, BMA Water District officials, engineers, and state and federal officials inspected the dam and disagreed about whether it was safe after finding seeping cracks. The state's top dam-safety engineer, Chau Vo, visited the dam later and concluded that he could not be 100-percent sure there was no danger. The Department of Public Safety issued a public warning that was relayed on television that evening by Bexar County judge Nelson Wolff. It resulted in the evacuations of Castroville and La Coste south of the dam. BMA officials were angered by the announcement and argued that the seeping cracks had always been there. They concluded that the dam would have stood 17 feet of water over the top because its limestone base would not erode. If the dam collapsed, an estimated 60-foot wave of water would rush down the Medina River to Castroville. In October 2004, the state determined that the dam could collapse if topped with six feet of water. Upgrades were ordered to be made. In 2011, construction began to improve and strengthen the dam to withstand an 11-foot overtop by floodwaters. (Courtesy of Sula Combs.)

Residents argued about whether the 2002 flood was worse than the 1978 flood. For those living upstream along the Medina River, the 1978 flood was considered more destructive. For lakeside residents, the 2002 flood proved to be more devastating. In 1978, the lake was hit with a 20-to-30-foot-high wall of water. The 2002 flood caused a slower gradual rise of water that resulted in higher water levels than in 1978, as the lake rose four feet above its previously recorded high level. The destructive force of floodwater is evident in these before-and-after photographs taken just two weeks apart. During a 1998 flood, the force of high waters along with flood debris toppled and sheared off 100-year-old cypress trees below Burt Spoerl's home upriver from Pop's Place on the Medina River. (Both images courtesy of Burt Spoerl.)

South Texas once again went into a cycle of drought beginning in 2005. By August 2006, over 90 percent of Texas was suffering from the drought, with 73 percent of the state in severe, extreme, or exceptional drought. While there was significant rainfall in 2007, the state returned to drought conditions in 2008. The drought of 2010–2011 was the worst since the great drought of the 1950s. With record-breaking high temperatures and prolonged periods of no rain, Medina Lake dropped to only 27 percent full. Water levels were 44 feet below normal. Though the lake had not dried up to the devastating levels of the 1950s, by 2011 its surface was only 35 percent of normal. Trucks can once again drive on the lakebed where boats once sailed. (Above, courtesy of Karen Downing Ripley; below, courtesy of Ron Bird.)

For those who work and live around Medina Lake, droughts are particularly devastating. The values of property owners' lakeside homes plummet, and business owners see a decline in customers as lake levels decline. The issue of who has rights over the water becomes more contentious as this precious resource gradually disappears. To see a once thriving lake become a dry lakebed is heartbreaking, and residents can only look to the skies and wish for the rains to come again. Above, trucks drive farther and farther to reach the shoreline in order to launch their boats; below, businesses that once were on the shoreline now sit above dry coves. (Above, courtesy of Roy Chancy; below, courtesy of Karen Downing Ripley.)

On rare occasions, snow comes to Medina Lake and creates a winter wonderland to be enjoyed ever so briefly. Life comes to a standstill as businesses close and children stay home from school. Above, a billboard for Camp Medina sits in a field after a rare snowfall in the 1940s. Below, Karen Ripley, Wayne Saunders, and friends explore Lakehills after the largest snowstorm on record hit in 1985 with over 18 inches of snow. The irony of posing next to a sailboarding sign was not lost on these winter explorers. (Above, courtesy of the Seekatz family; below, courtesy of Karen Downing Ripley.)

Seven

WHISKEY IS FOR DRINKING, WATER IS FOR FIGHTING

Medina Lake is a microcosm reflecting the world's growing dilemma over depleting water resources. Populations soar while water supplies dry up and water quality becomes polluted. Urban dwellers are set against rural dwellers as conflicting regulations lead to discord between competing interests over dwindling water resources. Water wars continue to prove the old Western adage that "whiskey's for drinking and water's for fighting!" The photograph shows dueling canoeists playfully jousting. (Courtesy of the Seekatz family.)

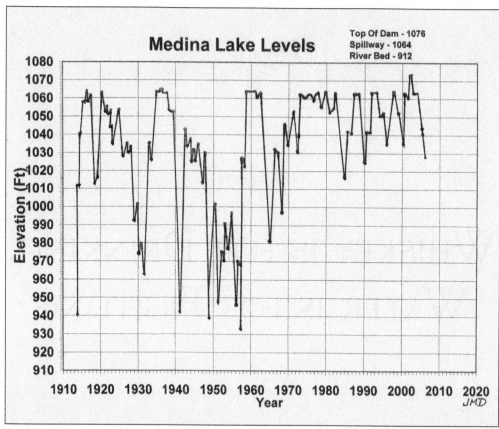

Medina Lake sits in a semiarid desert where there is often too much water followed by too little. Medina Dam was built to provide irrigation to farmers and profit for investors. When the lake is full, the farmers have bumper crops and businesses boom. Water levels in local wells are as high as property values and taxes. When the rains disappear and lake levels fall, so do the spirits of the farmers and business owners. (Above, courtesy of John Dale; below, courtesy of the Seekatz family.)

Medina Valley Irrigation Company (MICO) completed the dam in 1912. For many whose fertile river-bottomland was appropriated, the project was seen as an attack on individual property rights that allowed foreign investors to benefit from foreign labor over the confiscated lands of American ranchers. The lake began to fill before the final condemnation hearings were settled. A few ranchers in the flood zone fought against MICO, whose representatives testified that the company should not have to pay market value because it did not want to own the land below the level of the top of the dam (the 1084 line). MICO's people testified that they merely wanted an easement to flood the land; the landowners would retain ownership with the right to use the land to the water's edge. Pictured above is a cornfield from before the dam was built. Pictured below is the same area near Milligan's Cove, covered in water. (Above, courtesy of the Seekatz family; below, courtesy of Marlene Leibold Grotheus.)

Further delaying the development of the irrigated farms was the loss of foreign investment following Europe's entry into World War I. A catastrophic blow was suffered when Medina Dam's project manager, Dr. Frederick Pearson, and his wife, Mabel, were killed aboard the *Lusitania* when it was sunk by German U-boats; the Pearsons were traveling to Europe to raise additional investment money. (Courtesy of the Library of Congress.)

Following World War I, Medina Valley Irrigated Farms was purchased for $2.5 million to become San Antonio Irrigated Farms. Following receivership in 1930, Matt DuBose, mayor of Devine, persuaded the company to reduce the debt to $250,000. Securing a loan from the Reconstruction Finance Corporation, the project was saved. A public burning of the bonds was held in 1934. In 1950, Bexar-Medina-Atascosa Water Improvement District No. 1 (BMA) was formed and took over the assets. (Courtesy of Steve Bonahoom.)

Hardworking farmers, including those from the Oklahoma dust bowl, fought for their land despite drought and a bad economy. As the lake rose, the landowners above the dam had to adapt to a new way of life. Many knew how to raise crops and herd stock, but few knew how to profit from tourism. Many leased their lands to entrepreneurs who capitalized on the growing tourism business. Mico and Lakehills began to be populated with permanent residents who felt they had more than a weekend stake in the lake. To these new residents, Medina Lake was no longer just a recreation site; it was home. To the farmers whose dreams were realized below the dam, the lake's primary function was to supply irrigation waters, pitting them against the residents whose livelihoods and homes depended upon a lake with substantial water levels. Lakeside residents did not want to feel like trespassers who would have no say about the water. (Courtesy of Loy Ed Johnson Alanis.)

Investors of the Medina Dam project joined with influential San Antonio businessmen to claim the adjoining land around Diversion Lake for a private club, called Diversion Lake Club, which was later to become a development called Medina Ranch. Fishermen demanded access to the Medina River below the dam and to Diversion Lake. Following numerous suits, the Texas Supreme Court ruled that all Texans had the right to the river and Diversion Lake but not to the land around it. (Courtesy of Steve Bonahoom.)

The City of San Antonio, with its increasing population, looked to Medina Lake as a future water resource. Communities above and below the dam worked with San Antonio to implement the original plan to build a canal from the Guadalupe River to Medina Lake. When the city did not have the necessary funds, Canyon Lake was built in the early 1960s, ending hope for diverting Guadalupe River floodwaters to replenish Medina Lake. (Courtesy of Karen Downing Ripley.)

In 1966, the Medina Lake Betterment Association (MLBA) was formed to protect Medina Lake as well as resident rights. In 1977, following notification by the State of Texas to clean up the lake, BMA charged dock owners a $25 annual permit fee and outlawed houseboats, metal drums, and septic tanks located below the 1084 line. This conflict became known as the Houseboat Wars. While MLBA agreed to the need to control pollution, it protested against BMA charging waterfront-property owners fees to use the lake. (Courtesy of Kristina and Tom Fett.)

The Medina Lake Protection Association (MLPA) was formed in protest of BMA wasting water. MLPA charged that the BMA was misusing lake water to fill personal lakes below Diversion Dam. Following costly court battles in the early 1980s, the courts upheld that BMA had no regulatory authority above the dam. New state agencies, including the Texas Board of Water Resources and the Edwards Underground Aquifer, joined the Texas Parks and Wildlife Service in water-protection efforts. (Courtesy of the *Bandera Bulletin*.)

After a young woman slipped on the rocks at the spillway and died, BMA sought to close access to the road across the dam and spillway, which had been considered public for over 70 years. Lake residents took their fight to the Texas Supreme Court, which ruled that the dam roads were public and should remain open. In 1986, however, activists went to the Medina County Commissioners Court, which unanimously voted to close the road over the dam and spillway to public access. (Courtesy of Carol Smith.)

The State of Texas considers surface water from rivers and navigable streams to be the property of the citizens of Texas. All water purveyors, such as BMA, must have a permit from the state in order to sell water. BMA's original permit was for 66,000 acre-feet per year to be sold solely for irrigation. In 1987, BMA turned down an offer by Edwards Underground Water District to purchase BMA's water interests. (Courtesy of the BMA Water District.)

In 1992, BMA asked the Texas Natural Resources Conservation Commission (TNRCC) to change its permit to enable BMA to sell water to San Antonio via Bexar Metropolitan Water District (Bexar Met). The farmers used an average of 30,000 acre-feet of their total allotment of 66,000 acre-feet per year. According to former Lake Medina Conservation Society (LAMCOS) president Ralph Dresser, the organization formed in 1994 to protest BMA's effort to change its water permit in order to sell municipal water. Following extensive hearings with TNRCC, BMA agreed to grant Bandera County the right to purchase 5,000 acre-feet of water. In exchange, BMA agreed not to take more water from the lake after the level reached 1,035 feet above sea level (37 feet below the spillway) until the 400 miles of canals were lined and sealed to prevent losing three out of five gallons of water leaving the lake due to seepage, evaporation, and ungauged (stolen) use. The agreement was not reached when the LAMCOS membership voted against the mean pool conservation level of 1,035 feet above sea level, requesting instead that water not be taken below 1,050 feet. (Courtesy of Karen Downing Ripley.)

Lake Medina Conservation Society filed against the TNRCC and BMA in state district court on grounds that the application to change the permit use from irrigation to municipal use did not specify the kind and amount of use for each purpose. After lengthy court battles, a settlement was reached between BMA and Bandera County officials to permit BMA to sell only 20,000 of its 66,000 acre-feet per year for municipal water use with no mention of a mean pool conservation level. Many LAMCOS members were angry at county officials—including the Springhills Water District, who had agreed to the permit change in exchange for future water rights many believed they should not have to pay for. Many believed the county was best served keeping the water in the lake for residents whose wells often went dry as lake levels fell. The agreement also left Medina Lake with no mean pool conservation level, unlike other state lakes, increasing fears that there is no regulation to prevent drawing the lake dry and thus compromising not only residents' water wells but also reducing recharge of the Edwards Aquifer that supplies San Antonio. (Courtesy of Karen Downing Ripley.)

In 2002, BMA challenged 20 waterfront owners over their right to occupy property below the Elevation 1084, claiming it had ownership interest in most of the land at the level below the top of the dam. The Waterfront Property Owners Association (WPOA) formed and sued BMA in state court. The judge ordered the parties to mediate. BMA offered a settlement agreement asking property owners to give BMA a claim to the land and then lease it back from BMA for an annual fee. Fewer than 100 properties along the 110 miles of Medina Lake shoreline signed and consummated the agreement. Many who signed the agreement had homes situated below the level of the top of the dam and feared losing their homes if BMA sued them. The court ruled the agreement legally binding to those who signed. However, the judge said the agreement was in no way a precedent to force all property owners into the agreement. (Courtesy Karen Downing Ripley.)

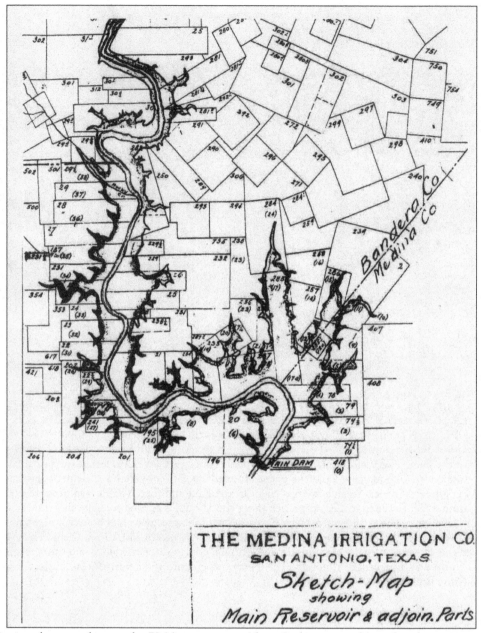

During the struggle over the BMA agreement, Alton Seekatz came forward with an original transcript from one of the condemnation hearings when MICO originally sought to gain easement rights along the Medina River for land that would be flooded with the construction of the dam. His grandfather Frank Seekatz, one on the last holdouts, had fought against MICO's inundation of his land. MICO did not want to pay fair market value for the land and made no claim of ownership to the land below the 1084 line, the level at the top of the dam. MICO representatives testified that they only wanted the right of easement to inundate the land with water, that Seekatz could use the land when it was not flooded, and that if the dam ceased to be then it would revert back to the original owner. BMA attorneys viewed the transcript as invalid, as it could not be used in court because it could not be proven to have been legally filed. (Courtesy BMA.)

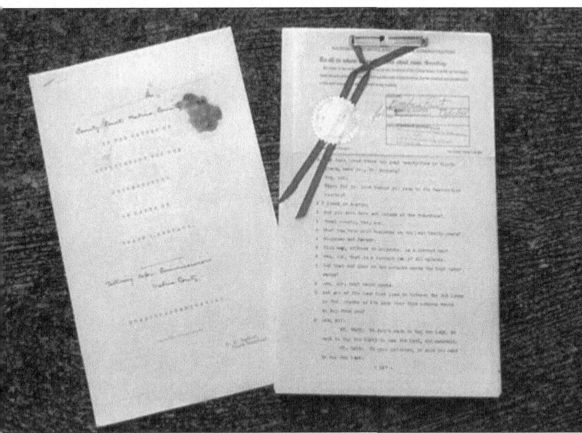

Joe and Kate Persyn, homeowners on Pebble Beach waterfront, began extensive research regarding the BMA agreement. They sought the original transcripts of the condemnation hearings for the rights the various property owners retained. They failed to find the Seekatz transcripts during their first trip to the National Archives regional office in Fort Worth. On their second visit, they pulled two document boxes, from before and after those registered as containing the transcripts, and found the lost testimony. These filed documents supported Alton Seekatz's claim that BMA did not own the land below the 1084 line. Nonetheless, the Waterfront Property Owners Association leadership accepted the BMA agreement. Many members of the WPOA disagreed with this decision, as it was against the wishes of many who had donated money to WPOA in opposition to the BMA agreement. (Courtesy of Karen Downing Ripley.)

As San Antonio's population increases, the city continues to expand toward Medina Lake. Mico is less than two miles from San Antonio's Extra Territorial Jurisdiction (ETJ). San Antonio recently secured over 1,000 acres near Turk's Head (above) on the Medina County side of the lake as an undeveloped area to protect the Edwards Underground Aquifer, the city's main water source. There is concern that the city may extend its ETJ to include communities around Medina Lake. Many Medina Lake residents fear being annexed by the City of San Antonio with its rules, regulations, and higher taxes. Mico and Lakehills have failed in attempts to incorporate because of reluctance by voters to pay new local taxes for services currently provided by their counties. They remain unprotected from future annexation by San Antonio and could lose their right to incorporate. Once in another city's ETJ, communities cannot incorporate without permission from that city. (Both images courtesy of Karen Downing Ripley.)

Lakehills' water and private property rights have been challenged by efforts to create rules that support special interests of one area of the county over that of Medina Lake. The Springhills Water District was formed in 1991 with powers as a river authority. The name was subsequently changed to Bandera County River Authority and Ground Water District (BCRAGD). The district's authority is established by state law and is charged with the distribution and protection of water in Bandera County. The district has often been a hotbed of controversy, as special-interest groups propose stringent water-use regulations in an effort to keep out development, sometimes at the risk of taking away their neighbors' individual property rights. "Grandfathering," "riparian right," and "vested interest" continue to be terms confusing to taxpayers and challenging to the board of directors. (Above, courtesy of Karen Downing Ripley; below, courtesy of Bandera County River Authority and Groundwater District.)

In 2010, Medina Dam received her first major face-lift in over 98 years. Construction crews began the $11-million projected repairs in December 2010 after altering the schedule to accommodate the breeding season of the golden-cheeked warbler. An interlocal agreement was implemented between the San Antonio River Authority (SARA), the Bexar Metropolitan Water District (Bexar Met), Edwards Aquifer Authority (EAA), Bexar County, the Texas Water Development Board (TWDB), and the Bexar-Medina-Atascosa Water Control and Improvement District (BMA), who all shared in the expenses and the decision-making process. The fact that Bandera County, Bandera River Authority and Ground Water District (BCRAGD), and Medina County were absent from the planning table caused some concerns. (Both images courtesy of Karen Downing Ripley.)

Medina Lake residents are aware of another threat to future lake levels. In 2011, the Edwards Aquifer Authority stated that 62,000 acre-feet of water for agriculture could be transferred for municipal use to utilities like the Bexar Met Water District if the owners were willing to lease and if municipal water utilities were willing to pay more than farmers for water. In 2011, Bexar Met came under fire for inherent inefficiencies, and customers voted to have it disbanded. As a result, Bexar Met's agreement with BMA for 20,000 acre-feet of water from Medina Lake could be transferred to the larger San Antonio Water System. Residents fear if additional water is taken from Medina Lake for municipal use as well as irrigation, water wells will dry up. At right, acreage shown under irrigation on October 10, 2011, has diminished dramatically over the years, leading to water being wasted in old canals. Below, dry waterfront property is pictured at lakeside on that same October 2011 date. (Both images courtesy of Karen Downing Ripley.)

Medina Lake's future water availability was strengthened in 2011 by a new law enabling water districts to manage the demand and availability of water with more flexibility. Texas State Legislature's Bill 332 reaffirmed groundwater as a property right based on the "rule of capture," which gives landowners ownership of the water below the surface of their property. The bill was originally written with groundwater as a "vested" property right, which would have conflicted with the ability of groundwater districts to protect a shared resource. The word *vested* was stripped from the bill, thus removing threat to the state's water supply. Had the change not been made, all landowners would have been entitled to as many wells as they wanted, and they could pump as much as they wanted. (Courtesy of Murray Walker of Allied Water Well Drilling.)

In 2011, BCRAGD and Bandera County worked with the United States Geological Survey to install a stream-gauge station on the Medina River to monitor floodwaters and provide a vital tool for flood emergency preparation. The satellite-linked station provides real-time, constant readings of water levels and the rate of river flow to emergency workers and residents and is easily accessed via the Internet. This is only a first step in flood warning, as additional gauges are needed to protect the entire county. (Courtesy of BCRAGD.)

A spin-off effort by LAMCOS is the Medina River Protection Fund, which holds an annual Medina River cleanup. Volunteers from around the state come to Bandera and gather tons of debris that floats down the river toward the lake. LAMCOS also creates public awareness programs on water issues and raises funds through grants to monitor the river's water quality. (Courtesy of Robert and Barbara Brichetto [pictured].)

In 2012, Medina Dam turns 100 years old. Following the success of the Medina Lake Preservation Society's (MLPS) 75th anniversary, the group will hold the Medina Lake Centennial Celebration, including all the communities that have a stake in Medina Lake both above and below the dam. Here, from left to right, Carol Smith, Panchita Thomson, Johnny Zinsmeister, and Betty Baxter celebrate the 75th anniversary of Medina Lake Dam in 1987. (Courtesy of Kristina and Tom Fett.)

Water does not come from a pipe in the ground. It takes many forms and is part of the Earth's cycle that sustains life. The lack or presence of water can divide people. It is only by coming together in the spirit of mutual benefit that people can hope to hold on to their water and their communities. (Courtesy of Karen Downing Ripley.)

Eight

TALL TALES, HAPPY TRAILS

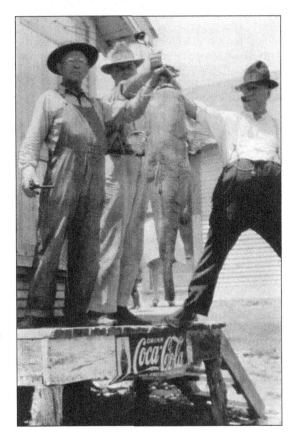

Medina Lake is a place where traditions run deep and the truth can sometimes be stranger than the tall tales that are told over a cold drink. Rumors of a giant catfish lurking beneath its surface and larger-than-life characters have given life at the lake a sense of humor as well as a sense of mystery. From the well-known to the regular folks who have graced its shores, Medina Lake has been both a home and an escape from the ordinary. (Courtesy of the Seekatz family.)

As an investor in the Thousand Trails Resorts, Roy Rogers came to visit the Medina Lake resort in 1984. When he arrived, he was picked up by a stagecoach driven by Kelly Scott (right) and Bob Malone. As the stagecoach made its way to the famed Spettel House at the resort, hundreds of fans ran alongside, cheering Rogers. Kelly Scott remembers that he felt like a "rock star" as the fans' adulation washed over them. (Courtesy of Kelly Scott.)

Everyone knew the "Admiral of the Lake," Panchita Thomson, who watched the dam being built as a child. Panchita befriended national columnist Heloise (Eloise Bowles), who owned a nearby lake house. In a poem written to her friend, Bowles said that Panchita was the "love and epitome" of Medina Lake because of her good deeds and charity work for the people of Medina Lake. (Courtesy of Kristina and Tom Fett.)

Though she may not have been the *Queen Mary*, the *Queen Elizabeth of Camp Medina* did sail for a time on Medina Lake. Setting sail from Camp Medina, the boat ferried 40 lucky passengers through the beautiful waters of the lake. The owner, F.A. Tallmadge, was so proud of his "luxury ship" that he posted the cost of the boat on its trailer: $6,500, a high price in the early days of the lake. (Courtesy of Chris and Debbie Heyen.)

Italian aviator Francesco de Pinedo caused quite a stir when he landed his plane, the *Santa Maria*, right on the lake's surface during his flight across four continents by request of Mussolini. Escorted by planes from Kelly Field in San Antonio, the voyager was met by government and military officials, giving the new lake its first international incident. (Courtesy of Marlene Leibold Grothues.)

"Let's go to the lake" has been the rallying cry for generations of South Texans. Little planning is required to make a fast escape through the winding roads into the cool hill country. Visitors can get high on life as the heady smell of cedar mixes with mountain laurel and the earthy scent of fish and lake. When temperatures soar, just "jump in the lake!" Pictured here, Tommy Adams defies gravity in 1966. (Courtesy of Tommy Adams.)

Pictured from left to right, Phillip Ford, Johnny Gaubatz, and Truman Spears, along with Ray Schoch (behind the camera) headed to Goat Hill Camp for this fishing trip in 1943. No one had a driver's license, but they scrounged up enough rationed gas, piled their gear into Truman's father's 1928 truck, and went to the lake. Their fun ended when Phillip got caught in the nose with a fishhook, and they had to head back to San Antonio to find a doctor. (Courtesy of Diane Spears.)

Fishing has always been popular at the lake. Generations have passed down their secrets about best time and place as well as proper gear and bait. Jim Gallagher learned a lot about fishing with his father, James D. Gallagher, long before he opened Jim's Rebait Tackle Shop on Park Road 37. Jim is pictured here with his father. (Courtesy of Jim Gallagher.)

Catching fish was just half the fun. Leslie Cox shows that frying them up was the real treat. Every fisherman has his own special recipe. While the men prepared the meat, the women brought delights from town—including baked beans, green bean casserole, lemon squares, and brownies followed by sweet tea and an occasional beer or three for the guys. (Courtesy of Gary Cox.)

Among the legends that surround the lake is the tale of those who are buried in the Medina Dam. For generations, it has been said the dam serves as a tomb for the unfortunate workers who were killed during its construction. In researching his book, Rev. Cyril Kuehne found no evidence among the death certificates of those who died that would support this rumor. Kuehne felt that if an ill-fated worker had fallen into the concrete, he would have been removed for a decent burial. The morbid rumor did not deter the many visitors who were fortunate to visit the top of the dam. The view was spectacular, and the power and the strength of the dam were intoxicating. Today, the dam is closed to the public. Burt Spoerl and Karen Ripley are pictured below. (Above, courtesy of Marlene Leibold Grothues; below, courtesy of Karen Downing Ripley.)

Medina Lake has served as a respite for several famous and notorious people. Among the elite who built second homes on the lake's bluffs were Marion Koogler Atkinson McNay. San Antonio's most famous art patron, Marion enjoyed this lake house with her third husband, Dr. Donald Atkinson, though the marriage was short-lived (1926 to 1936). McNay arranged for her San Antonio home to become the city's first art museum upon her death. (Courtesy of the McNay Art Museum Library and Archives.)

The lake home of Henry B. Gonzalez Jr. has been the setting of many family get-togethers and holidays. Henry's father is a San Antonio legend, serving as a US congressman representing Texas's 20th congressional district from 1961 to 1999. The congressman and his wife enjoyed spending time on the lake with their children—including his son, Congressman Charlie Gonzalez—and grandchildren. (Courtesy of Karen Downing Ripley.)

In the mid-1990s, Allan and Kim Smith, at their own expense, began treating Medina Lake to a tremendous Fourth of July fireworks show. Hundreds of boats gather in Elm Cove around Tiki Island at dusk to enjoy the display. Their elaborate display rivals those of any city and has become a treasured tradition for the community. (Courtesy of Allan and Kim Smith.)

Nothing tastes better after a hot day floating on an inner tube than ice-cold watermelon—especially when the grown-ups let you eat to your heart's content and don't care when you get it all over your clothes. You don't even have to take a real bath—they just throw you back into the lake. But be careful. The mythical dragon, Anidem, who snatches naughty children, may be waiting. Pictured here are the Agee grandchildren and friends. (Courtesy of Howard and Nina Agee.)

The history of Medina Lake is the story of triumph and conflict. While the good guy in the white hat, Roy Rogers, graced the lake, legendary gambler Champ Carter met his demise by a 12-gauge shotgun. It has been a place of laughter and mystery, where the sightings of a lost pet monkey have matched sightings of elusive Monkee Michael Nesmith, whose mother Bette bought a lake home with earnings from her invention, Liquid Paper. While the economy, weather, politics, and the passage of time may temporarily erode the lake, her prospects for a bright future remain with her people, the ones who call her home, and with the children who will be entrusted to carry on and preserve the essence of Medina Lake. Pictured above is a young Burgin Johnson at Goat Hill Camp in the 1940s; below, the Harrises' grandkids sit on a log that washed up following the 2002 flood. (Above, courtesy of Burgin and Valli Johnson; below, courtesy of Bobby and Patty Harris.)

Visit us at
arcadiapublishing.com

CPSIA information can be obtained
at www.ICGtesting.com
Printed in the USA
BVOW04*0930131117
500281BV00018B/486/P